T0344189

STUDENT
MENTAL
HEALTH

STUDENT MENTAL HEALTH

{ Purvi Gandhi }

CORWIN

1 Oliver's Yard
55 City Road
London EC1Y 1SP

CORWIN
A Sage company
2455 Teller Road
Thousand Oaks, California 91320
(800)233-9936
www.corwin.com

Unit No 323-333, Third Floor, F-Block
International Trade Tower, Nehru Place
New Delhi 110 019

8 Marina View Suite 43-053
Asia Square Tower 1
Singapore 018960

© Purvi Gandhi 2024

Apart from any fair dealing for the purposes of research, private study, or criticism or review, as permitted under the Copyright, Designs and Patents Act, 1988, this publication may not be reproduced, stored or transmitted in any form, or by any means, without the prior permission in writing of the publisher, or in the case of reprographic reproduction, in accordance with the terms of licences issued by the Copyright Licensing Agency. Enquiries concerning repro-duction outside those terms should be sent to the publisher.

Editor: Delayna Spencer
Editorial assistant: Harry Dixon
Production editor: Sarah Sewell
Copyeditor: William Baginsky
Proofreader: Neil Dowden
Indexer: Melanie Gee
Marketing manager: Dilhara Attygalle
Cover design: Wendy Scott
Typeset by: C&M Digitals (P) Ltd, Chennai, India
Printed in the UK by Bell and Bain Ltd, Glasgow

Library of Congress Control Number: 2023948713

British Library Cataloguing in Publication data

A catalogue record for this book is available from the British Library

ISBN 978-1-5296-7240-4 (pbk)

To Papa. Your love and courage light my path.

TABLE OF CONTENTS

ABOUT THIS BOOK   IX
ABOUT THE SERIES   XI
ABOUT THE AUTHOR   XIII
ACKNOWLEDGEMENTS   XV

INTRODUCTION   1

1. WELLBEING: HOW CAN IT BE ENHANCED IN THE
   CLASSROOM?   5
2. FINDING STRENGTH: HOW CAN AN APPROACH FOCUSING
   ON INDIVIDUAL STRENGTHS ENHANCE STUDENT
   WELLBEING?   17
3. STRESS: WHY DO SOME STUDENTS EXCEL UNDER
   PRESSURE WHILE OTHERS STRUGGLE?   31
4. MOTIVATION: HOW CAN INTRINSIC MOTIVATION BE
   DEVELOPED TO STRENGTHEN MENTAL FITNESS?   45
5. SOCIAL INFLUENCE: HOW CAN GROUP PRESSURES
   INFLUENCE WELLBEING?   59
6. ASSESSING WELLBEING: LOCATING STUDENTS AND
   PROGRESSING THEM ALONG THE WELLBEING GRADIENT   73

REFERENCES   87
INDEX   93

{ ABOUT THIS BOOK }

Student mental health is a huge issue in the education sector, and due to overwhelmed mental health systems greater pressures are placed on teachers to offer pastoral support to students. This book is packed with practical strategies to help teachers with supporting their students.

- Authored by an expert in the field
- Easy to dip in and out of
- Interactive activities encourage you to write into the book and make it your own
- Read in an afternoon or take as long as you like with it!

Find out more at
www.sagepub.co.uk/littleguides

a little guide for teachers

{ ABOUT THE SERIES }

A LITTLE GUIDE FOR TEACHERS series is little in size but big on all the support and inspiration you need to navigate your day-to-day life as a teacher.

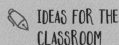 IDEAS FOR THE CLASSROOM

HINTS & TIPS

REFLECTION

NOTE THIS DOWN

www.sagepub.co.uk/littleguides

ABOUT THE AUTHOR

Purvi, also known as Vi, brings more than 20 years of experience as an educator, having taught in both state and independent schools in the UK. She holds an MA in Psychology and later earned an MBA in Educational Leadership. Before her teaching career in the UK, Purvi primarily served as a psychotherapist in the USA, specialising in child and adolescent mental health.

Throughout her career, Purvi has engaged in numerous research projects, yielding improvements for both colleagues and students. Many of these projects have pinpointed the crucial social and emotional aspects of learning, integral to enhancing teaching effectiveness. As a practising educator, Purvi understands the importance of evidence-backed, effective strategies that can be embedded into practice. Over the past decade, she has dedicated herself to researching, implementing, and evaluating diverse practical strategies for promoting mental health in education.

One notable initiative, that was effective in her context, involved the creation of a tailored Year 9 Positive Psychology Curriculum, drawing inspiration from the works of Seligman, Duckworth, Zimbardo, and Chamene. This curriculum delivered a toolkit designed to bolster students' psychological wellbeing. Quantitative and qualitative data collected to measure the impact confirmed the benefits of the course. The techniques in the toolkit enhanced students' sense of purpose and reinforced relationships resulting in a positive effect on academic outcomes.

Inspired by feedback from numerous colleagues, students, and parents who suggested making the course's insights available to all teachers, Purvi has authored this guide for teachers. It is her hope that educators will find this resource valuable in fostering wellbeing in schools.

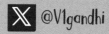 @V1gandhi

WWW.LINKEDIN.COM/IN/PURVI-GANDHI-AKA-VI-GANDHI/

ACKNOWLEDGEMENTS

Heartfelt thanks to Nirav for his unwavering support and patience, and to Alpa, Misha, and Bhavesh, I cannot express how much your support impacts and uplifts me. To my children, Kareena and Anjali, whose laughter brings joy to my work, your presence is a constant reminder of what truly matters.

Deep gratitude to the educators who contributed their invaluable perspectives. A special mention to WomenEd, Deb, Delayna, Paul, James, and Vicky; thank you for believing in me.

To my inspiring colleagues, you make every day brighter. To all my students (especially that Year 9 class), your curiosity keeps me humble and creative. You matter – more than you know. Thank you.

INTRODUCTION

Mental health is an integral component of health and wellbeing that underpins our individual and collective abilities to make decisions, build relationships and shape the world we live in.
World Health Organization, 2022

The mental wellbeing of our students must no longer be an afterthought; it is a matter of paramount importance. The challenges of mental illness often begin early, well before adulthood (Independent Mental Health Taskforce to the NHS in England, 2016). In 2021, it was reported that nearly 40% of children between the ages of 6 and 16 had experienced a deterioration in their mental health since 2017 (NHS Digital, 2021). This figure was derived from a comprehensive study assessed the mental health status of children and adolescents during the Coronavirus (COVID-19) pandemic. It not only investigated the changes in mental health since 2017 but also delved into the impact of the pandemic on

various aspects of their lives, including family dynamics, education, and access to support services. Furthermore, NHS Digital revealed that in 2022, children's wellbeing continued to decline, with approximately 5 of every 30 likely to grapple with a mental health issue. The causes for this decline are multifaceted; they include a variety of factors ranging from negativity about school, possibly exacerbated by the disruption to education caused by the pandemic, to broader issues such as the environment, inequality, and geopolitical tensions. For educators, it has become imperative that we place supporting the mental health of students at the very core of our educational practice if we wish to equip them for fulfilling adult lives.

Educators can play a critical role in enhancing the mental health of students. As a teacher, you have a unique opportunity to positively impact the lives of many children. Creating a classroom that is supportive of mental health is crucial – this is the challenge that stands before us. This book aims to provide teachers with evidence-backed, practical resources for supporting student mental health. It will explore key theories and studies, offering examples of how these concepts can be applied in the classroom.

In this book, terms such as 'good mental health' and 'mental/ psychological fitness' will be used interchangeably with 'wellbeing'. Many definitions and theories surround wellbeing, but a useful definition is the one offered by the World Health Organization (WHO, 2022) that it is a state 'in which the individual realizes his or her own abilities, can cope with the normal stresses of life, can work productively and fruitfully, and is able to make a contribution to his or her community'. This conceptualisation helps us to break down wellbeing into manageable constructs that will be used to structure this book.

Chapter 1 explores one theory of wellbeing and its application in the classroom. Chapter 2 delves into recognising strengths so that individuals can realise their own abilities. Chapter 3 explores stress and coping strategies, while Chapter 4 looks into motivation to work productively and fruitfully. Chapter 5 discusses the impact of social influences and examines the role of community in mental health.

Lastly, Chapter 6 describes the wellbeing gradient and identifies further resources where more information can be found.

The focus of this book is *not* on mental illness – it is not a replacement for counselling or other forms of support that some children may need for their psychological health. Rather, it is a starting point for teachers to encourage their students to thrive in school. The book offers a toolkit of practical ideas that can make a positive difference in the classroom. While at first it may feel strange to try out new strategies, I encourage you to keep an open mind and reflect on your experiences. Keep a journal of your reflections because it can help you to evaluate which strategies work best for your students and for you.

 REFLECTION

What does the term 'mental health' mean to you?

In what ways do you encourage the mental health of your students?

What are you hoping for from this book?

It is important to remember that good mental health requires regular practice and effort, much like physical fitness. The goal of this book is to help teachers create healthy classroom environments that prioritise student wellbeing. By focusing on building their students' mental fitness, teachers may also see a positive impact on their own wellbeing.

Ultimately, this book is a journey of discovery and growth. It is a resource for teachers who want to make a difference in the lives of their students. So, enjoy the journey, the wonderful discoveries, and the memories that come with it.

CHAPTER 1
WELLBEING
HOW CAN IT BE ENHANCED IN THE CLASSROOM?

This chapter covers:

- The PERMA (Positive Emotions, Engagement, Meaning, Relationships, and Accomplishment) theory of wellbeing
- Evidence-backed strategies that improve wellbeing by developing each element of PERMA
- Examples of how these strategies can be adapted to nurture a classroom culture that values wellbeing

> *The key to a healthy life is having a healthy mind*
> Richard Davidson, 2012

What is 'wellbeing'? How do we experience it in ourselves and how do we know when others have a high degree of wellbeing? A great deal of research has been undertaken to answer these questions. To offer a simple introduction to the topic in this book, I have selected one theory of wellbeing that was proposed by psychologist Martin Seligman. Seligman's theory offers a useful framework I have applied in various classrooms, including my subject lessons and with tutor groups, over the last decade (Seligman, 2011).

There are five fundamental elements to the theory: Positive Emotions, Engagement, Relationships, Meaning, and Accomplishment, and with those elements comes the acronym PERMA. We can enhance each of these components through specific techniques to create a supportive environment for our students.

THE PERMA THEORY OF WELLBEING

POSITIVE EMOTIONS

 IDEAS FOR THE CLASSROOM

Gratitude journal: Ask students to write down three things they are grateful for every day for 21 days. Each item can be big or small but cannot be repeated on subsequent days of the activity.

Shawn Achor, author of *The Happiness Advantage* (2011), found that initially people write down the major things they are grateful for – like family, food, and home. But with passing days, the items get more granular. People start scanning the world for things to be grateful for and this is the aspect of the practice that makes it so effective. When we actively look for what is right in the world, we start to develop a mindset that allows us to be more resourceful and resilient.

For example, a teacher used the exercise in the following way with their tutor group:

1. The group agreed to try out the 21-day gratitude journal exercise after talking about the psychological research and benefits of the activity.

2. The group were given a small exercise book to use as their gratitude journal.

3. The journals were laid on their desks each morning and students were given three minutes to write the three things they are grateful for.

4. Sometimes the tutor looked through students' journals (with their permission) to ensure that they were following through with the exercise.

5. At the end, the effects of this activity were discussed. Most of the students said that they looked forward to writing in their journals because it made them more appreciative of the good things in their lives.

Another benefit of undertaking this exercise was that it helped the tutor to understand her tutees better. When she read the journals, the tutor was better able to understand the things each student appreciated in their lives.

 REFLECTION

How do you enhance positive emotions in your classroom?

A study by Lyubomirsky et al. (2005) found that practising gratitude exercises can increase happiness. Additionally, listening to uplifting or inspirational music can be a useful motivational tool (Juslin and Sakka, 2019). These studies show that simple practices like gratitude exercises and music selection can positively impact one's wellbeing.

All emotions have value in our lives. Experiencing emotions like happiness, joy, and gratitude are considered to be positive. This element suggests that by exposing ourselves to situations where positive emotions arise naturally, we can enhance our wellbeing. That does not mean that we ignore emotions considered to be negative such as anger or jealousy. Instead, Seligman suggests we should not only acknowledge them but also process them constructively. By doing so, we develop our ability to deal with difficulties.

ENGAGEMENT

When students are fully absorbed in meaningful and enjoyable experiences, they experience what psychologist Csikszentmihályi calls 'flow' – the state of complete immersion and engagement. Such activities foster a sense of satisfaction and enhance wellbeing.

Research has shown that engaging in meaningful and enjoyable activities, such as creative projects or games, can increase students' motivation and interest in learning (Shernoff and Csikszentmihalyi, 2009).

Engagement is also improved when students' skill levels and the challenge levels of tasks are perfectly aligned (Csikszentmihályi, 1990).

 REFLECTION

How do you enhance engagement in your classroom?

RELATIONSHIPS

Building meaningful relationships is at the heart of fostering a sense of wellbeing. In our classrooms, it is vital to create a sense of belongingness and connection for our students to thrive.

A study by Battistich et al. (2004) found that promoting positive relationships in the classroom, such as through cooperative learning activities, can increase students' sense of connectedness and belonging.

 ## IDEAS FOR THE CLASSROOM

Foster positive relationships in the classroom by promoting teamwork, group discussions, and cooperative learning activities. Acknowledge students' unique strengths and highlight them when an opportunity arises. Actively pointing these out not only supports the individual student but also helps the rest of the students see these strengths.

Here is a suggestion for an exercise to apply this strategy:

- Members of a class are each given a piece of paper with their name written at the top of the page but otherwise the page is blank.

- They pass the sheet to the person sitting next to them. The recipient of the page is asked to make a kind and thoughtful comment about the person whose name is on the paper.

- The sheet of paper is then passed onto the next person and so on until it comes back to the owner.

- The outcome of the exercise is that each student ultimately receives a sheet of paper filled with positive comments from their peers.

I tried this with my Year 13 class (and included myself in the circle). It was a fantastic experience for the class to strengthen relationships. I keep my sheet of paper in my memory box and look at it when I need a boost of positivity.

(Continued)

- *Make time to speak to your students to find out more about them*. Share a little about yourself (appropriate details only). Decide to have two ten-minute conversations with each one of your students over the course of the term.

- *Teach and model listening skills*. Really listening (not just to the words, but also what's behind the words – the emotions) builds empathy. Students are taught how to read and write, but they also need to develop the crucial skill of listening to build social connections. To teach our students to listen better, we can provide opportunities to practise the skill in the classroom. One effective technique to enhance listening abilities has been developed by Julian Treasure (Treasure, 2011), an expert in communication. This is the RASA method which consists of four steps:

  1. *Receive*: Be fully present and attentive when receiving the speaker's message.

  2. *Appreciate*: Show respect and appreciation for the speaker's perspective and feelings. Use noises like 'hmm' and 'oh'.

  3. *Summarise*: Demonstrate understanding by summarising the key points of the conversation.

  4. *Ask questions*: Engage in meaningful dialogue by asking relevant and thoughtful questions.

By teaching and modelling these listening skills, educators can empower their students to become better communicators and empathetic individuals.

 REFLECTION

How do you enhance positive relationships in your classroom?

MEANING

Having a purpose helps individuals focus on what is important in the face of significant challenges or adversity (Seligman, 2011). Activities that are misaligned with our goals/values can make us feel 'unbalanced' whereas those that are in line with our goals reinforce our sense of purpose.

A study by Vansteenkiste et al. (2009) found that helping students find meaning and relevance in their learning can increase their intrinsic motivation and engagement in the classroom.

 ## IDEAS FOR THE CLASSROOM

- Find out what your students value individually. What is important to them? Help them to find purpose and meaning in their learning by relating lessons to their interests and goals. Then offer opportunities for them to make connections between their learning and real-life situations.

- Let students know that the attitudes and behaviour they bring to lessons have an impact on others because they (the student) matter. For example, if they decide to be disruptive, then their choice will have an impact on others. Similarly, if they decide to develop kindness or teamwork, then it will make a difference to others around them. This is because their attitudes and choices matter.

When discussing this concept with my students, I openly expressed my deep commitment to my role as their teacher, stressing its purpose. I made it clear that, due to our limited time together, I aimed to create a meaningful and purposeful classroom environment in line with my values. Collaboratively working towards my goal of becoming the best teacher possible

(Continued)

fostered this sense of purpose for them. Consistently reinforcing this message led my classes to realise my sincerity. As I strengthened my sense of purpose, I observed improvements in my own wellbeing. Additionally, when my students recognised the impact of their thoughts and actions on others, including me and their peers, it not only made them feel valued but also instilled a sense of purpose.

 REFLECTION

How do you foster a sense of purpose in your classroom?

ACCOMPLISHMENT

Achieving important and meaningful goals gives us a sense of pride and can improve our wellbeing.

Research has shown that setting and achieving meaningful goals can increase students' sense of competence and self-efficacy, leading to greater motivation and engagement (Locke and Latham, 2002).

 IDEAS FOR THE CLASSROOM

- Think about creative ways to celebrate student achievements, specifically their effort.

- Encourage students to set goals that are SMART – specific, measurable, achievable, realistic, and time-bound (Falecki et al., 2018). Goals can also be set using the WOOP framework – Wish, Outcome, Obstacle, and Plan (Oettingen, 2012).

Posing questions such as 'What does success look like for you and how can we work together to find it for you?' can help students focus on realistic and achievable goals for themselves whilst knowing they are supported. Such questions can be used to target intervention based on what the student needs. They facilitate the creation of an environment where successes, no matter how big or small, are recognised.

 REFLECTION

How do you help your students set meaningful goals?

Seligman (2011) also recognised the concept of 'vitality', which is taking care of one's physical health for good mental health. Although this is not an inherent part of the PERMA theory, it is important to also recognise that sleep, exercise, and nutrition are necessary for wellbeing. These factors contribute significantly to students' overall mental health.

Cultivating each of these elements can increase our psychological resources, leading to a life of greater mental health and happiness. By incorporating the elements of the PERMA theory into classroom practices, teachers can support students in developing healthy habits. These can not only contribute to their overall wellbeing but also help to create a supportive classroom environment where students feel engaged in their learning.

Remember that every classroom is unique, and adapting these techniques to suit the needs and interests of your students is crucial. It is also important to note that teachers are not mental health experts. If the students in your care are struggling with mental health difficulties, it is important to follow your school's policies for making appropriate referrals to obtain the intervention of mental health professionals.

NOTE IT DOWN

Map your PERMA

By deciding to support your students' wellbeing, you also commit to looking after your own wellbeing. Use the questions below to reflect on your own wellbeing.

How would you describe your wellbeing? Use PERMA to help frame your thoughts.

Positive emotions: What makes you feel good?

Engagement: What activities do you get completely absorbed in?

RELATIONSHIPS: WHAT RELATIONSHIPS BRING YOU JOY AND SUPPORT? HOW DO YOU NURTURE THEM?

MEANING: WHAT LARGER PURPOSE DO YOU FEEL DRAWN TO?

ACCOMPLISHMENTS: WHAT WOULD YOU LIKE TO ACCOMPLISH IN THE NEXT WEEK, MONTH, AND YEAR?

WHAT ELEMENTS OF PERMA ARE YOUR STRONGEST? WHERE COULD YOU GIVE MORE ATTENTION TO REALLY FLOURISH?

CHAPTER 2
FINDING STRENGTH

HOW CAN AN APPROACH FOCUSING ON INDIVIDUAL STRENGTHS ENHANCE STUDENT WELLBEING?

This chapter covers:

- The notion of being 'seen' as having importance for student wellbeing
- Examples of how using an approach to identify individual strengths in the classroom allows the creation of a positive learning environment
- The idea that helping students to develop their strengths enhances their ability to overcome difficulties and empowers them to build mental fitness

Being 'seen' by teachers and classmates holds immense significance for students because it enhances students' self-esteem and motivation to engage in the learning process.

WHAT DOES BEING 'SEEN' MEAN?

Feeling seen is a subjective and nuanced concept that can vary from person to person. However, it can be described as the experience of being recognised, acknowledged, and understood by others in a way that validates one's thoughts, feelings, and identity (Pineda, 2022). It involves the perception that others are paying attention to you. And being seen generates a feeling that one's emotions, needs, and perspectives are genuinely understood, which can foster a sense of connection, empathy, and validation.

'Seeing' involves multiple acknowledgements, such as understanding, belonging, and respect, which play a pivotal role in shaping a student's sense of self and overall wellbeing. Conversely, when students do not feel seen, feelings of neglect and isolation can take hold, impacting their mental health and academic performance. When this happens over time, they may start feeling that they don't matter, which can set them on a downward emotional spiral. Their self-esteem takes a hit, and they may find it tough to reach out for help. Feeling 'invisible' even taints how people see the world, making them believe that their needs won't be met or that nobody cares.

In the classroom, 'seeing' can be done through various means such as:

- *Supporting the needs of students*: To help students feel seen on an interpersonal level, teachers can build connections in a wide variety of ways. Examples include greeting them at the classroom door when they arrive, pronouncing their names correctly, asking about their day, sharing in their joy, and providing emotional support when they need it.

- *Validating students' feelings and perspectives*: By highlighting the value of each student's perspective, teachers set the tone for inclusivity. When teachers demonstrate attentive listening, using phrases such as 'I understand that you feel...' or 'it's okay to feel...', they express empathy and ensure that students feel seen. Feedback can also be a tool for acknowledging students' efforts. Teachers can validate their students' attempts as they focus on improvement. By following up on students' previous contributions, teachers can show that they value and remember them.

- *Representation of diversity in lessons*: For example, using students' names in worksheets or using classroom examples from a diverse range of people. Representation fosters connection and understanding among different communities.

 ## HINTS AND TIPS

Use seating plans and/or name tags at the start of the academic year to quickly learn the names of your students.

 ## REFLECTION

Take a moment to reflect on your own childhood. Can you recall a teacher who made you feel truly seen and valued?

If so, give a name and description of that teacher. Try and recall some specific behaviours the teacher exhibited to make you feel seen.

By genuinely seeking to understand each other, we can make others feel valued and important, which is something that everyone deserves. In what ways do you make your students feel 'seen'?

Seeing and appreciating students for what they're good at boosts their confidence, helps them connect better, and keeps them motivated to do their best. When we focus on their individual strengths, it makes them feel valued and more excited about learning. In this book, the word 'strengths' is used to mean anything that a student *excels* in, *enjoys,* and gets *excited* about (Galloway et al., 2020). It also includes character strengths or character traits. 'Character strengths' refers to universally valued personality traits and behaviours that encompass our capacity for helping ourselves and others. When expressed, they promote positive effects for us and those around us (Peterson and Seligman, 2004).

By building on existing strengths rather than focusing on compensating for deficiencies, students experience better outcomes for enhancing their wellbeing. This approach is known as the strengths-based approach. It is a framework that places emphasis on identifying, using, and developing a core set of strengths that each student possesses. While acknowledging the existence of weaknesses, this approach harnesses the power of students' strengths to overcome areas of difficulty, driving them to grow holistically.

CHARACTER STRENGTHS

Character strengths are organised into traits that fall under six broad virtue categories: wisdom, courage, humanity, justice, temperance, and transcendence.

Wisdom and Knowledge	Temperance	Courage
Includes:	Includes:	Includes:
Creativity	Forgiveness	Bravery
Curiosity	Humility	Honesty
Judgement	Prudence	Perseverance
Love of learning	Self-regulation	Zest
Perspective		
Justice	Humanity	Transcendence
Includes:	Includes:	Includes:
Teamwork	Love	Appreciation of beauty and excellence
Fairness	Kindness	Spirituality
Leadership	Social intelligence	Gratitude
		Hope
		Humour

One way to help students identify their own character strengths is by showing them this list, teaching them about what each one means and asking them to identify which ones they identify with. You can ask them to get their friends and family to help identify the top strengths of a student. On the other hand, you could use a more systematic approach by using the validated Values in Action (VIA) youth survey which can be found on the Authentic Happiness (2023) website of the University of Pennsylvania. The survey is a personal strengths test that identifies an individual's top character strengths from a list of 24 traits, providing insights for personal growth and development.

 REFLECTION

To identify your top strengths, take a look at the 24 character strengths in the Values in Action survey and identify which ones resonate with you the most? Ask your family and friends which ones they recognise in you.

Alternatively, you can take the VIA Survey of Character Strengths test for adults.

What are your top strengths?

How do you use your strengths in your life to contribute to your wellbeing, specifically, your relationships, achievement, and enjoyment of life?

Identifying strengths is not an attempt to establish a set of strengths that is fixed for an individual for the rest of their life. Rather, it represents what is strong in you at a particular point in time. Although they are an enduring aspect of the character of a person, strengths can change over time. It is important to recognise that children's strengths will grow in number and nature as they continue to develop.

CHARACTER STRENGTHS IN THE CLASSROOM

By understanding and applying their strengths, students can improve their emotional regulation, relationships, academic performance, and overall life satisfaction (Linley et. al., 2010). Therefore, teachers should encourage students to be aware of how they can use their strengths to overcome adversity (Brownlee et al., 2012).

These are five ideas for bringing character strengths into the classroom.

CLASSROOM DISPLAYS

- Display posters of your students' strengths. You can try different variations depending on what is suitable for your context. Perhaps you could create a display that showcases your students' strengths. If you want your students to feel confident about sharing their own strengths, you could get them to make a poster of their own strengths. Alternatively, a good way to build relationships in your class is to get students to create a display of each other's strengths. This can make the classroom feel more inclusive, nurturing a sense of belonging.

- Display the character strengths of inspirational personalities juxta-posed with your students and their character strengths. This can have a powerful impact on students' motivation. For example, it can help them see that when they show curiosity in their science work, it is the same character trait exhibited by inventors like the Wright brothers. Or they may realise that Ellie Simmons' self-regulation and persever-ance in swimming are the same traits needed to excel in maths.

DEVELOP AND PRACTICE NEW SKILLS

Set aside dedicated strengths-based learning time during which students can individually develop their strengths. For example, for a maths assignment, you can say, 'Andy, this is your chance to exercise your perseverance muscle even more by having a go at dividing these fractions!' or 'Lily, this is your opportunity to develop leadership skills by writing a how-to guide to help students divide fractions'.

DEVELOP GREATER APPRECIATION

The SEA framework (Spot, Explain, Appreciate) can help students identify strengths in action (Niemiec and McGrath, 2019). The first step is to spot the strength. Then encourage students to explain what they observed and justify their reasoning. Finally, have them appreciate the value that the particular strength brings.

 REFLECTION

Use the SEA framework to spot the strengths of the people around you. Write your reflections below:

Spot:

Explain:

Appreciate:

OFFERING PRAISE

Instead of solely focusing on grades for effort and achievement, also reward character strengths. For instance, when a student gracefully handles not being picked for a team, praising their *perspective* can be encouraging and supportive. Notice and reward *courage* when a nervous student successfully completes a class presentation. Be specific in your praise – for example, 'I noticed how Rico *persevered* with the maths question on multiplying fractions. It was fantastic to see that he kept trying even though he found it difficult. That quality – of sticking with it – will help him in many areas of life, not just in maths.'

TARGET SETTING

Set targets for development that intertwine with character strengths. Frame targets as 'doing *what* by *how* to develop *which* character strength'. For example, set a goal *to improve debating skills* by *arguing for a viewpoint that you disagree with* that will further develop *perspective*. Or to *improve writing skills* by *writing a journal every day* for a month to develop *perseverance*.

 REFLECTION

What specific activities could you ask your students to undertake to nurture their strengths?

DEVELOPING STRENGTHS

When teachers and classmates acknowledge a student's strengths and their achievements, it creates a sense of belongingness for the student. Equally important is when students recognise their own achievements. Having the confidence to celebrate one's achievements does not come easily to everyone. It needs to be learned. When done well and in a supportive environment, it can boost confidence. Consciously cultivating strengths allows people to develop a bank of psychological resources that they might need to cope with life's challenges.

 IDEAS FOR THE CLASSROOM

A useful tool to help students to frame their successes is the STAR method (National Careers Service, n.d.). The STAR method involves breaking the story of an achievement into four components: Situation, Task, Action, and Result.

- *Situation*: Set the scene and give the necessary details for the anecdote.

- *Task*: Student describes what their task/responsibility was in that situation.

- *Action*: Student explains exactly what steps they took to address it.

- *Result*: Student shares the outcomes that their actions achieved.

 CASE STUDY

Examples of students using the STAR method – Tanvi, Year 8

Situation: We had this history project where we had to work in a group and make a news report about an important event from the past. I was excited about it because I love history, but I was also a bit nervous because I didn't know everyone in my group very well. Anyway, our teacher gave us the task, and we had to decide who would do what in the report. It was tough because we all had different ideas.

Task: I took the lead and suggested that we divide the work based on our strengths. I'm good at research, so I volunteered to find all the historical facts and information. Another girl in my group was great at writing, so she took charge of the script. Then, we had someone who was good with presentations, so they handled the video editing and making it all look good.

Action: We had to work together and compromise on some stuff, but we did it! It wasn't always easy and we had disagreements, but we managed to figure it out by listening to each other's ideas. It was not exactly how I wanted it, but it was still good. We practised a lot, and everyone did their part really well.

Result: On the day of the presentation, we felt a mix of nerves and excitement. But when we showed our news report to the class, they loved it! Even the teacher was impressed!

I think this whole project helped me develop the character strength of teamwork. We all brought our strengths together, communicated, and supported each other to make an awesome news report.

(Continued)

When I started to encourage my students to journal and then share their achievements out loud (including times they exercised their character strengths), I noticed they found it a little awkward at first because they felt that it was 'bragging' and 'not really a big deal'. But with practice, they became increasingly confident about sharing their achievements. Moreover, they started to enjoy it. The activity was also a great opportunity to practise the RASA listening technique (mentioned in Chapter 1) whilst one of their classmates spoke about their achievements. It was an effective way of creating a positive learning environment.

It's not bragging if you can back it up
Muhammad Ali

 ## REFLECTION

Use the STAR method to reflect on a time when you applied your strengths to meet a challenge.

In what ways can you use the STAR method in your classroom? What are the benefits and challenges?

S

T

A

R

To enhance the mental fitness of your students over time, the following must be recognised:

- *Intention*: Teachers must be intentional about harnessing students' strengths. When character strengths are embraced, behaviour and wellbeing improve in schools (Galloway et al., 2020).

- *Action*: There is a difference between insight and action. Knowing about the strengths-based approach is not enough; making it a regular part of your teaching practice is necessary. It needs to be constant by drawing attention to and developing students' character strengths during their school experiences – from assemblies to tutor time, playgrounds, school corridors, individual subject classrooms, and even conversations with parents (Corcoran and Whitehead, 2021).

- *Model*: Teachers are role models. Learning about and developing our own strengths will allow us to lead by example so that our students also work on developing their character.

- *Boundaries*: Mental health in schools and classrooms is promoted by having high expectations of all children with clear boundaries. Everyone should know what is expected of them and understand the rewards and consequences of certain choices (Weare, 2013). This structure creates psychological safety.

According to the self-determination theory proposed by Ryan and Deci (2000), psychological wellbeing hinges on fulfilling three essential human needs: competence, autonomy, and relatedness. Utilising a strengths-based approach within the classroom effectively addresses all three of these needs. Initially, as students recognise and celebrate their strengths, they develop a sense of competence. As their confidence develops, they can then be given autonomy and encouraged to use their strengths to take on challenges.

NOTE IT DOWN

Cultivating character strengths can provide a pathway for better mental health. This activity can be done with your students but have a go at it yourself first.

Here are five ways to develop curiosity.

1. Watch a show that you would not normally choose.

2. Ask five people a question each day for a week.

3. Try food or listen to music from a different part of the world.

4. Take part in an activity that you would not normally choose.

5. Research a topic that you are interested in finding out more about.

Make up or look up five ways to develop another strength, such as courage. Set yourself realistic goals to develop a strength of your choice, write your reflections below.

CHAPTER 3
STRESS
WHY DO SOME STUDENTS EXCEL UNDER PRESSURE WHILE OTHERS STRUGGLE?

This chapter covers:

- The definition and nature of stress
- How stress may manifest in the classroom
- Valuable resources for teachers to support students to successfully navigate stressful situations

It is important for teachers to understand the impact of stress on the mental health of students and provide them with effective strategies to manage and mitigate its harmful effects.

WHAT IS STRESS?

It is an undeniable part of life. Stress is an inherent aspect of the human experience, arising as a natural response to challenging or threatening situations. Within the body, it causes the release of hormones like cortisol and adrenaline. These hormones trigger a cascade of physiological events, including increased heart rate, heightened alertness, and redirection of energy to essential functions. Emotionally, stress can often manifest as feelings of anxiety, fear, or unease.

When the perceived demands of a situation are greater than the perceived resources to meet those demands, the situation can be considered stressful
Lazarus et al. (1985)

Stress = perceived demands are greater than (>) perceived resources

EXAMPLES IN THE CLASSROOM

Demands made by an exam > revision materials, time, knowledge, skills = stress

Demands to complete a piece of coursework > lack of reasonable adjustments, poor access to SEND resources = stress

Expectations to achieve a certain grade > capabilities in that subject = stress

EXAMPLES OUTSIDE OF THE CLASSROOM

Household expenses > monthly income = stress

Physical demands of climbing a mountain > lack of training = stress

 REFLECTION

What might a stressful situation look like in your classroom?

What demands do your students face in the classroom?

What resources are available to them?

Stress is a normal and natural part of life, and not all stress is bad. In fact, positive stress, known as 'eustress', can be beneficial as it spurs us on to develop the resources needed to handle challenges or reduce the stressors themselves. It can help us to pay attention, heightening our focus and boosting our creativity, which leads to innovative thinking to solve problems. Moreover, stress can nudge us to reach out to others, which can strengthen relationships.

However, it is important to be aware of chronic stress, which occurs when stress persists over an extended period. Chronic stress is strongly linked to various physical and mental health issues. Here is where the Yerkes-Dodson law comes into play. This is a psychological concept suggesting that there is an optimal level of stress which leads to peak performance. Too little stress can lead to underperformance, whilst too much stress, especially when it is chronic, can have harmful effects on our wellbeing. Striking the right balance between stress and performance is essential for maintaining overall health and effectiveness in managing life's challenges.

THE STRESS RESPONSE

The stress response is evolutionary. It activates the body's 'fight or flight' mechanism, preparing us to confront or flee from perceived threats (McGonigal, 2013). We can also sometimes 'freeze' as a response to stress when neither fighting nor fleeing is an option.

 REFLECTION

Think back to the previous reflection point, when the demands are greater than the resources available to your students, what behaviours do they exhibit?

Consider how the stress response may manifest itself in the classroom.

Fight	• Arguing with others • Acting out • Screaming/yelling • Fighting • Irritability • Restlessness	Your observations:
Flight	• Missing lessons • Not doing the work set • Daydreaming • Avoiding others • Refusing to participate • Difficulty concentrating	Your observations:
Freeze	• Not answering questions when called upon • Looking startled when asked to participate	Your observations:

It is essential for teachers to be attuned to these signs and respond empathetically and effectively to support the mental health of students. This is not to say that poor behaviour should be accepted. On the contrary, good classroom management, which includes having clear expectations, routines, lesson structures, and sensitive planning, is fundamental in creating a safe and supportive classroom environment. This is because such practice provides students with the resources (social, psychological, academic, etc.) to learn in your classroom.

MANAGING STRESS

When you change your mind about stress, you can change your body's response to stress. McGonigal, 2013

In this section of the chapter, three crucial skills for stress management will be discussed:

1. Recognising and harnessing the power of thoughts

2. Fostering emotional agility

3. Creating space between feeling and responding

RECOGNISING AND HARNESSING THE POWER OF THOUGHTS

Kelly McGonigal, a health psychologist, has conducted research that challenges the conventional notion that stress is entirely harmful. How we think about stress influences how we respond to it. McGonigal argues when the stress response is perceived as a natural part of life, it helps us to meet challenges and enables growth. Viewing stress as a coping resource can lead to improved focus and resilience.

Students' perception of the demands placed on them together with the resources they possess influence how they feel and act. Thoughts, emotions, and behaviours are interconnected. Cognitive psychologist Albert Ellis's ABCD model is useful to help students understand this concept: C (emotional consequences) stem not directly from A (an adverse situation) but from B (one's beliefs about the adverse situation). As teachers, we can gently help students to D (dispel) unhelpful beliefs about the challenging situation or themselves. The idea is that when we think about a situation in a different way, it allows us to feel and behave differently. This is known as cognitive restructuring or cognitive reappraisal (Ellis, 1991). A study done by researchers Banks and Zionts in 2009 found that this approach allowed students to better understand their feelings and emotions so that they can be better learners.

AN EXAMPLE

Situation (A): A student is asked to participate in a challenging PE lesson.

Belief (B): The student believes that she will look 'stupid' in front of others, that she will make a mistake and that she will let others down.

Consequence (C): The student will be reluctant to participate, leading to a lack of confidence and increased fear of failure.

Dispelling (D): Teachers can gently challenge the student's beliefs by creating a safe environment in which they feel supported by reminding them that their effort will be worth it if they learn something from the experience. Teachers can also offer additional support or resources to help the student improve their skills. By doing so, the student may start to view the challenge as an opportunity to learn and grow rather than as a threat, which can lead to reduced anxiety and improved performance.

If a student's internal self-talk is harsh and critical of themselves and/or others, then it may result in distress. Once identified, these thought patterns can be counteracted by empathy, connecting with others' emotions and perspectives, and building positive relationships. Empathy is defined as part of a family of positive emotions including compassion, gratitude, and forgiveness – it removes barriers and expands the capacity for self-love and love for others (Chamine, 2012).

The role of empathy in learning is significant as it helps students understand and connect with the material they're studying. It allows them to step into others' shoes, to see the world from different perspectives. For instance, in history, understanding the motivations behind events becomes easier with empathy. Moreover, it helps students connect with people from diverse backgrounds, which is valuable in a global society. Empathy is a crucial aspect of social–emotional learning, aiding students in building relationships, communicating effectively, and resolving conflicts. Learning goes beyond simply holding knowledge; it involves understanding the human and emotional aspects of information to gain new perspectives.

Positive relationships are fundamental to supporting students to restructure their thinking. Without a good relationship, any attempt to do this can make matters worse. It is important to use techniques (such as the ABCD model) sensitively, being careful to acknowledge students' feelings and thoughts. A good rule of thumb is to be empathetic and non-judgemental.

FOSTERING EMOTIONAL AGILITY

Even a happy life cannot be without a measure of darkness, and the word happy would lose its meaning if it were not balanced by sadness.
Carl Jung (1921)

In our society, there is a tendency to avoid or suppress difficult emotions. According to psychologist and author Susan David (2016), children should be taught emotional agility to better navigate this world. Emotional agility involves accepting all emotions, even the uncomfortable ones, rather than pushing them away, denying their existence, or masking them with inauthentic positivity. By helping our students to be curious and non-judgemental about emotions (not seeing them as 'good' or 'bad'), we can help them to gain self-awareness and make choices that are aligned with their values and goals. This emotional self-regulation skill is an important aspect of wellbeing.

David explains that often when people feel a supposedly negative emotion such as sadness or anxiety, they self-identify with the emotion and in the process 'lose themselves'. For example, phrases such as 'I am sad' (or 'anxious' or 'stressed') suggest that emotions are part of a person's identity. Instead, phrases such as 'I notice that I am feeling sad' (or 'anxious' or 'stressed') create distance between an emotion and a reaction. Such reframing allows us to use our emotions as data points before deciding on a course of action.

Once you have identified the emotion you are feeling, get granular – go beyond the umbrella term to describe what you feel using two other words. This way you can more accurately identify what you are feeling. For example, If you're feeling sad, getting granular might involve identifying specific emotions within that broader feeling. For instance, you might realize that you're feeling 'lonely' due to missing friends or loved ones and 'disappointed' because of an unexpected setback. By recognising that your sadness encompasses feelings of 'loneliness' and 'disappointment,' you can better address the underlying causes and manage those specific emotions more effectively.

 HINTS AND TIPS

It may be a good idea to help students develop a glossary of emotions. See the figure below for an example based on the emotional granularity checklist (David, 2021).

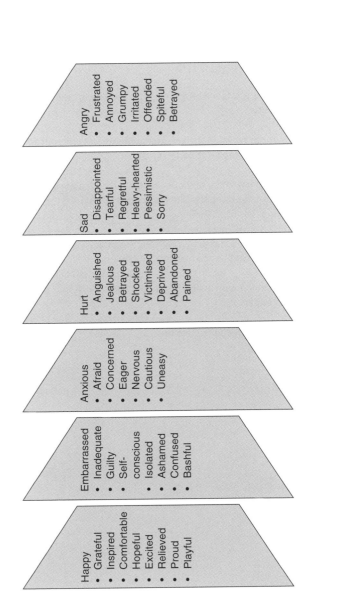

Happy
- Grateful
- Inspired
- Comfortable
- Hopeful
- Excited
- Relieved
- Proud
- Playful

Embarrassed
- Inadequate
- Guilty
- Self-conscious
- Isolated
- Ashamed
- Confused
- Bashful

Anxious
- Afraid
- Concerned
- Eager
- Nervous
- Cautious
- Uneasy

Hurt
- Anguished
- Jealous
- Betrayed
- Shocked
- Victimised
- Deprived
- Abandoned
- Pained

Sad
- Disappointed
- Tearful
- Regretful
- Heavy-hearted
- Pessimistic
- Sorry

Angry
- Frustrated
- Annoyed
- Grumpy
- Irritated
- Offended
- Spiteful
- Betrayed

 # REFLECTION

Next time you feel a tough emotion like anger, embarrassment, or anxiety:

1. Try to focus on the emotion without judgement (see it as neither good nor bad – it just is).

2. Go beyond the obvious to identify the feeling at a more granular level (use the emotion checklist).

3. Once you have identified your feelings at a deeper level, consider what your emotions are telling you about what is important to you about your values.

4. Decide on an action (no matter how small) that is aligned to your values.

5. Jot down your reflections.

While trying to control our emotions can lead to harmful effects on mental health, managing them and choosing our response can be empowering.

CREATING SPACE BETWEEN FEELING AND RESPONDING

Creating space between feeling and responding is advantageous as it promotes emotional regulation, leading to better decision-making and reduced stress. Mindfulness is a powerful tool that can used for this purpose. In classrooms, it can enable students and teachers to develop a non-judgemental acceptance of emotions, create space for thoughtful responses, and embrace discomfort with compassion. By incorporating mindfulness into their lives, students can develop a deeper understanding of themselves leading to greater wellbeing. There are many apps that students can use and short online videos available for all age groups that teachers can use. For example, some of my students have found the Australian (non-for-profit) Smiling Mind app very beneficial whereas some of my colleagues have found the classroom activities 'Reflect' feature in Microsoft Teams useful to build a positive learning culture.

 IDEAS FOR THE CLASSROOM

Here is a simple practice:

1. Find a relaxed, comfortable position. You could be seated on a chair or on the floor on a cushion. Keep your back upright, but not too tight, hands resting wherever they're comfortable, tongue on the roof of your mouth or wherever it's comfortable.

2. Notice and relax your body. Try to notice the shape of your body and its weight. Let yourself relax and become curious about your body seated here – the sensations it experiences, the touch, the connection with the floor or the chair. Relax any areas of tightness or tension. Just breathe.

3.   Tune into your breath. Feel the natural flow of breath – in, out. You don't need to do anything to your breath. Not long, not short, just natural. Notice where you feel your breath in your body. It might be in your abdomen. It may be in your chest or throat or in your nostrils. See if you can feel the sensations of breath, one breath at a time.

4.   Stay here for five to seven minutes. Notice your breath, in silence. From time to time, you might notice that you are getting lost in thought. When this happens, without judgement, gently bring your attention back to your breath.

5.   After a few minutes, once again notice your body, your whole body, seated. Let yourself relax even more deeply and then offer yourself some appreciation for doing this practice.

6.   Notice how you feel.

Mindfulness can help us attune to our thoughts, feelings, or bodily sensations that suggest we're getting anxious or angry, enabling us to manage those emotions before they get the better of us. Teachers can build in shorter practices into the classroom routine.

An alternative to mindfulness practices is doing PQ reps, which are exercises that increase 'positive intelligence quotient' to build self-regulation and self-command, according to Shirzad Chamine, an influential mental fitness guru. PQ reps are any activity (repetitions/reps) that shifts your attention to your breath, your body, or your environment for at least ten seconds. PQ reps can be:

• Tactile, like rubbing fingers together gently and trying to feel the ridges of the fingers.

• Visual, like looking at any single thing and noticing every detail about it – shadow, light, texture, depth.

- Auditory, like listening as far away as you can and noticing all aspects of that sound, then listening inside your body for your heartbeat.

When a negative emotion is experienced, acknowledge it quickly and do some PQ reps. Focus on your breath, rub your fingers together, and pay exquisite attention to the sensation, then when the mind is a bit clearer, ask yourself, 'What gift or opportunity can come from this situation?' This is called the 'sage' perspective – the belief that every situation can be converted into a gift or an opportunity.

Looking for the gift, no matter how small, in each negative experience helps reframe the thoughts associated with the experience.
Shirzad Chamine

NOTE IT DOWN

FOR THE REST OF THE DAY (OR WEEK) IF YOU COME ACROSS
A CHALLENGING SITUATION, TAKE A BREATH, FOCUS YOUR
ATTENTION, AND ASK YOURSELF WHAT GIFT OR OPPORTUNITY
CAN COME OUT OF THIS SITUATION.

JOT DOWN YOUR REFLECTIONS HERE:

CHAPTER 4

MOTIVATION

HOW CAN INTRINSIC MOTIVATION BE DEVELOPED TO STRENGTHEN MENTAL FITNESS?

This chapter covers:

- Explanations of how wellbeing and motivation are interlinked
- Various theories of motivation that are relevant in the educational setting
- Practical ways of developing intrinsic motivation

According to the World Health Organization (2022), a state of wellbeing includes being able to work 'productively and fruitfully'. Motivation refers to the psychological processes that drive the effort of an individual towards achieving specific goals so that they can work in such a manner.

FULFILMENT OF NEEDS

There are many useful psychological theories of motivation that can be applied to education. For example, Abraham Maslow's hierarchy of needs is a theory which suggests that people are motivated to fulfil their needs in terms of priorities (Maslow and Lewis, 1987). The highest priorities are the most basic physiological needs, such as the need for food and water, followed by a need for physical safety. Once these are fulfilled, there comes the need for belongingness before progressing to higher-level esteem and self-actualisation needs – to develop and reach one's potential (Al-Harthy, 2016). A simple example of this in the context of the classroom is that if students don't have their more basic needs of sufficient rest, adequate nutrition, or stability in friendships they are more likely to disengage from academic matters.

For the wellbeing of our students, we should be aware of their needs and vigilant when those needs are not being met. Although this chapter discusses many aspects of the needs of students, it is important to state that teachers must adhere to statutory guidance such as *Keeping Children Safe in Education* (KCSIE) which is regularly updated by the Department for Education (DfE) in England. The other nations of the UK have similar safeguarding guidance. At the time of writing the most recent versions were published in 2023. The guidance points to the expectations of teachers.

Teachers hold a crucial role in their students' lives, requiring vigilance, attentive observation, listening, and and active education. Some ways that the curriculum can be used to support students' needs include:

- Instil the importance of fundamental self-care practices, including a healthy diet, regular exercise, and sufficient sleep.

- Take steps that help students to keep themselves safe (offline and online) and know what to do if they feel unsafe.

- Take opportunities to develop intra-personal skills (like self-awareness and emotional regulation) and nurturing interpersonal skills (such as effective communication and collaboration).

Maslow's Hierarchy of needs is a useful theory because it can support teachers in developing specific strategies to address fundamental human needs. Having an understanding of different types of motivation can help teachers to spur students on to reach their potential.

TYPES OF MOTIVATION

Motivation can be categorised into two main types:

1. *Extrinsic motivation*: This stems from external factors such as rewards, recognition, or avoiding punishment. People with extrinsic motivation perform tasks to attain a specific outcome or to gain something external, rather than for the inherent enjoyment of the activity.

2. *Intrinsic motivation*: This type of motivation comes from within an individual. It is driven by personal interests, enjoyment, and a sense of satisfaction derived from the activity itself. Intrinsic motivation leads people to engage in tasks for the inherent pleasure and satisfaction they provide.

Extrinsic and intrinsic motivation are interconnected – one can enhance the other. For instance, if a student enjoys painting (intrinsic), they might be more likely to participate in an art competition for a prize (extrinsic). On the other hand, getting an extrinsic reward for a task can sometimes lead to increased intrinsic interest in that task. For example, a reading challenge with extrinsic rewards like small prizes may initially motivate students. However, as they delve into books, they might develop an intrinsic passion for reading, drawn in by compelling stories or new-found knowledge. Therefore, it is important for teachers to utilise both types of motivators. But it is also important to achieve a balance. While intrinsic motivation tends to lead to sustained engagement and higher quality of work, external rewards can provide initial incentives. However, overreliance on external rewards can eventually diminish intrinsic motivation, so it's essential to create an environment where intrinsic motivation is nurtured.

 REFLECTION

How do you motivate your students to be productive and fruitful? Do you use a balance of extrinsic and intrinsic motivators?

DEVELOPING INTRINSIC MOTIVATION

Helping our students to become intrinsically motivated will help them to thrive. Having a sense of curiosity and solving meaningful problems provides a release of dopamine, a neurotransmitter that plays a key role in the brain's reward pathway. It makes us feel good, so we strive for the feeling again.

Research evidence points to the following factors that relate to the development of intrinsic motivation in students:

- Finding their work meaningful (Bawuro et.al., 2019)

- A growth mindset (Dweck, 2008)

- Having choices, feeling capable and supported (Deci and Ryan, 1985)

MEANINGFUL WORK

Meaningful work, in a school context, is the subjective sense of importance that emerges when students feel aligned with their learning. It is the personal acknowledgement of how their efforts contribute to their sense of purpose. Simon Sinek, leadership expert and author of the best-selling book *Start with Why* (2011), argues that knowing your purpose or your 'why' is an essential starting point for meaningful work. It is essential for intrinsic motivation.

REFLECTION

Why do you do the work that you do? How does this link with your values?

I am intrinsically motivated to bring mental health into the core of my practice because I am convinced that doing so brings long-term benefits to my students. This work aligns with my values and enhances my wellbeing. Similarly, helping students to understand the purpose of their learning and linking that with their values can be hugely motivating.

IDEAS FOR THE CLASSROOM

To get an idea of what your students value, you could try the following activity:

1. **Give students question prompts to get them thinking about their values:**

   - **Describe an incident or event from which you learned a lesson the hard way.**

   - **Who has been most important in your life in helping you establish your values? Please explain.**

   - **What are the three most important values you think will be important to encourage in your children one day?**

   - **What is the one rule that you believe is important to live your life by?**

2. **Follow up students' statements with questions to help them think more deeply about their answers. For example, what makes these qualities worth admiring and worth following? Why are these qualities or values so important to you?**

3.   **Ask them to write a reflective essay. Instruct them to reflect on the past year, both in and out of school. Advise them to include details of what they consider to be the values or principles by which they want to live their lives. And importantly, ask them to state why.**

4.   **Then ask them to commit to living by their principles. Throughout the school year, you can have them reflect on what they wrote and committed to.**

The above activity was sourced from a book called *Urban Dreams: Stories of Hope, Resilience and Character* (Elias et al., 2007). The editors published a moving collection of reflective essays by primary and secondary school students who wrote about their core values and the guiding principles that shape their actions. This gave their teachers an opportunity to understand what motivated them.

I assigned this task to my Year 9 students and was moved by their stories. I was able to learn so much about them – about what was important to them and why. This assignment helped me to make a deeper connection with my students so that I was better able to teach them in a way that was meaningful for them. For example, one of my students wrote about his older sister's cancer diagnosis and treatment during the Covid pandemic. He was in Year 9. He wrote about the impact that this had on his family. He spoke about the helplessness that he felt. From his experience, he realised that it was important for him to make a difference – to feel helpful. His values included supporting his own family and being there for the families of others who were going through a difficult time. These values guided his decisions. It motivated him to engage in everything from responding constructively to feedback to participating in community volunteering programmes. In lessons, I made clear links with how the classroom activities related to his goals and values. During GCSE results day, after opening his envelope, he and his mum were holding back tears because he was one step closer to a career in healthcare.

Values alone are not enough to reach long-term goals. Students also benefit from 'grit'. Angela Duckworth, a researcher internationally renowned for her work on the topics of grit and achievement, has defined grit as a combination of *passion* and *perseverance* (Duckworth et al., 2007). Her research has suggested that grit is a key predictor of success and achievement.

 REFLECTION

In her TED Talk 'The power of passion and perseverance', Angela Duckworth shares stories and research findings to illustrate the power of grit in various contexts, such as education and professional success. Watch her talk (www.youtube.com/watch?v=H14bBuluwB8) and write down your reflections here.

Duckworth finishes her talk by suggesting that one way to cultivate grit is by developing a *growth mindset* in students. This type of mindset promotes a sense of purpose and resilience, positively impacting psychological wellbeing.

GROWTH MINDSET

A growth mindset is the belief that abilities can be developed through effort and learning. Embracing a growth mindset encourages students to see challenges as opportunities for development. This enhances their motivation to learn because they are not held back by a fear of failure. They have realised that failure is a necessary part of the learning process.

> *I've missed more than 9,000 shots in my career.*
> *I've lost almost 300 games. Twenty-six times, I've been*
> *trusted to take the game-winning shot and missed.*
> *I've failed over and over and over again in my life.*
> *And that is why I succeed.*
> Michael Jordan

 IDEAS FOR THE CLASSROOM

Teachers can foster a growth mindset in the classroom by:

- *Teaching children about the tremendous plasticity of the brain – its ability to grow and change with effort and practice*: For instance, jugglers are not born knowing how to juggle. With effort and practice, they make new neural pathways so that they can throw and catch juggling balls beautifully. Their physical body does not change, but their brains do. Like an optical illusion, this concept becomes so obvious to many students once it has been pointed out!

- *Sharing inspiring stories of individuals who have overcome challenges through effort, practice, and self-regulation*: The *Rocky* film series is a great example where the titular character overcomes adversity through these behaviours stemming from a growth mindset. It is incredibly important to emphasise to children that abilities and capabilities are not fixed traits but can be developed.

- *Offering specific feedback that focuses on effort, progress, and strategies employed rather than solely on outcomes or grades*: This highlights the importance of the learning process and encourages students to value the journey rather than being solely outcome oriented.

- *Using classroom displays that show the growth mindset in action*: I had a student who wrote and rewrote the same essay seven times. Each time she took on the feedback provided and made her essay better than before. With her permission, I displayed all seven essays to demonstrate the growth mindset.

SELF-DETERMINATION THEORY (SDT)

A useful idea for stimulating intrinsic motivation is described by the SDT. Developed by Richard Ryan and Edward Deci (2017), this theory emphasises the importance of intrinsic motivation as a result of meeting three basic psychological needs: competence, autonomy, and relatedness.

- *Competence*: The feeling of being skilled. It involves seeking challenges and practising activities to enhance one's skills. It is not only about the level of ability but also the *belief* in being able to achieve.

- *Autonomy*: The feeling that actions taken are under the individual's control, the experience of choice and willingness. Doing something because you want to, not because you have to.

- *Relatedness*: The feeling of being connected to others. Supportive relationships can contribute to the development of abilities and promote success.

 # IDEAS FOR THE CLASSROOM

IDEAS FOR THE CLASSROOM FOR THE DEVELOPMENT OF COMPETENCE

- **Provide clear instructions, scaffolded learning experiences, and appropriate challenges that match students' abilities:** Ensure that work is accessible for *all* students irrespective of their level.

- **Explicitly teach students the cognitive science of learning:** This is an effective way for students to take ownership of their own learning. For example, educating them about concepts like working memory, cognitive load theory, dual coding, and retrieval practice can boost their confidence and academic performance (Gandhi and Outwaithe, 2023).

IDEAS FOR THE CLASSROOM FOR THE DEVELOPMENT OF AUTONOMY

- **Provide choice:** Offer students meaningful choices within the learning process, such as selecting topics, tasks, or learning methods. This allows students to feel a sense of ownership and control over their learning, promoting their autonomy.

- **Encourage self-reflection:** Offer opportunities for students to reflect on their own learning process, set goals, and evaluate their progress. Guide students in developing metacognitive skills to monitor and regulate their own learning.

IDEAS FOR THE CLASSROOM FOR THE DEVELOPMENT OF RELATEDNESS

- *Acknowledge perspectives*: Encourage valuing and considering other students' thoughts, ideas, and perspectives in decision-making. Encourage open dialogue and active listening to foster a sense of relatedness and shared ownership of the learning experience.

- *Promote collaboration*: Create opportunities for cooperative learning, peer interaction, and collaborative projects. Encourage students to work together, share ideas, and learn from one another, which foster a sense of relatedness and social support.

Where students are supported by others, have choices, and feel capable of making progress, they experience greater positive emotions and achievement. If teachers emphasise the joy and inherent value of the learning process rather than rely solely on external rewards or punishments, they will give students the tools to be productive and fruitful in life.

NOTE IT DOWN

What motivated you in school?

Who were your most motivational teachers? Why?

What did they do in their classroom to motivate you?

What steps can you take to build:

Competence

Autonomy

Relatedness?

Watch Rita Pierson's (2013) TED Talk 'Every kid needs a champion' (www.ted.com/talks/rita_pierson_every_kid_needs_a_champion?language=en). Jot down your reflections here.

CHAPTER 5
SOCIAL INFLUENCE
HOW CAN GROUP PRESSURES INFLUENCE WELLBEING?

This chapter covers:

- What social influence is
- Some examples of how group pressures might manifest themselves in the classroom
- What teachers can do to help their students positively influence their school community

It takes a village to raise a child.
African proverb (referenced in Reupert et al. 2022)

Social influence is about how others influence our attitudes and behaviours. Humans are inherently social beings, interconnected with others. Understanding social influence is key to empowering our students and guiding them to resist harmful group pressures. Whether it's conforming to fit in or seeking validation in uncertain situations, we must help students navigate these challenges and choose prosocial behaviours over harmful ones. Prosocial behaviours are ones that benefit others such as being helpful, considerate, cooperative, and contribute to a positive learning environment.

CONFORMITY

Plenty of social psychological evidence shows that when people stand out from the crowd, they can feel awkward and vulnerable because of the strong drive to fit in and to belong. In fact, our urge to fit in is so powerful that people tend to give in to conformity even when they know that the rest of the group is wrong. In a classic study by Solomon Asch, a social psychologist, naïve participants (who sat among a group of actors that were in cahoots with the researcher) were asked to judge the length of a line. In critical trials, where the actors gave obviously wrong answers, 32% of Asch's participants also gave the wrong answer despite knowing that it was incorrect. Asch concluded that people conform for two main reasons: they want to fit in with the group (normative influence) and they believe the group is more informed than they are (informational influence).

A good way of helping students, especially younger children, understand this concept is using the story of the 'The Emperor's New Clothes'.

In this story, a pair of swindlers convinced an Emperor that only 'stupid' people couldn't see the special cloth from which they would make a garment for the Emperor. As the Emperor and his subjects did not want to appear foolish, they all stated how wonderful the non-existent cloth was. This story illustrates how conformity can lead people to pretend they see or believe something that isn't true out of fear of social repercussions or a desire to fit in. Even though it's a natural human inclination to conform, it's vital to stay aware, notice these situations, and have the strength to resist conformity when it contradicts our sense of what's right.

DEINDIVIDUATION AND BLIND OBEDIENCE

When we are part of a group, there is a chance that we can lose our own identity and conform to the social role of the group. This is called deindividuation. For example, in his (in)famous study, social psychologist Philip Zimbardo gave psychologically healthy university students roles of either prisoners or guards in a mock prison. All the students knew that they were part of a psychological study in which they were role-playing. Despite this, the study had to be abandoned within six days when the 'guards' became abusive and the 'prisoners' became emotionally distressed with many of them blindly obeying the demeaning orders of the guards. Zimbardo concluded that the power of social influence can be so great that people can conform to their social roles even when it goes against their own moral principles.

Blind obedience can also be a concern, particularly when the perceived authority figure is malevolent. Of course, obedience is necessary in schools, but obedience without question can be dangerous.

Although we are hard-wired to be influenced by others, in some situations following the crowd can be detrimental to our mental health. Below are some examples of conformity, deindividuation, and blind obedience in the classroom.

Conformity	During a class discussion, a student might have a different opinion from the rest of the class on a controversial topic. Instead of expressing their unique viewpoint, they conform to the majority perspective to avoid potential conflict or judgement. This conformity prevents diverse perspectives from being discussed thus threatening wellbeing.
Deindividuation	Some students might become part of a larger group dynamic during a group project and lose their sense of individual responsibility. They might slack off or contribute less because they feel less accountable in a group. This can result in an unequal distribution of effort and negatively impact the overall project outcome.
Blind obedience	In a classroom setting, a teacher may ask students to complete an assignment that seems too challenging or inappropriate for their grade level. Some students might blindly obey the teacher's request without questioning its appropriateness or expressing their concerns. This blind obedience can lead to feelings of frustration, anxiety, and a lack of motivation to learn.

 REFLECTION

Think of a time when you were negatively influenced by group pressure. What happened? How could you have resisted the pressure to conform?

Teaching our students to be confident when handling socially difficult situations is important so that they can effectively negotiate harmful social pressure. Confidence develops from knowledge and experiences. Giving our students the tools to resist pressure (such as communication skills, assertiveness skills, seeking support, using emotional agility to determine values-led action, and developing character strengths) is a key part of supporting their mental fitness so that they can make a valuable contribution to society.

In schools, the community is an invaluable asset, brimming with opportunities to build strong relationships. Thriving communities cultivate wellbeing, which in turn nourishes 'well societies'. The wellbeing of your students is intricately linked to the overall health of the classroom community. Students with higher wellbeing actively contribute to a positive classroom atmosphere, demonstrating empathy and kindness to their peers. Their improved focus and engagement in learning create a more conducive environment for learning. Students who prioritise their mental health become role models and inspire others to do the same, setting the stage for a collective commitment to wellbeing.

PROMOTING PROSOCIAL BEHAVIOURS IN SCHOOLS

These are some of the ways teachers can encourage prosocial behaviours in the classroom:

- *Celebrate individuality and diversity to foster a culture of respect for differing perspectives*: Celebrate each student's unique strengths and qualities to reduce the risk of deindividuation within the classroom. By nurturing a culture that values diversity, students can thrive as individuals, building their sense of identity and self-worth.

- *Have open discussions about peer pressure, conformity, and the importance of making independent decisions based on their values*: Encourage students to speak up and ask questions.

- *Establish safe reporting channels, in line with school policy, for raising concerns about behaviours or people that make students feel uncomfortable*: Ensure that students know what to do if they feel the social pressure to do something that goes against their wishes/values. Continually raise awareness of and improve systems to ensure the safety and welfare of the school community.

- *Encourage students to develop a range of possible solutions to social dilemmas and reflect on the consequences of different actions*: This could also be done through role-play, which can allow students to practise responding to peer pressure in a safe and controlled environment whilst gaining the confidence to resist social pressure. By seeing people as individuals rather than mere groups, we cultivate a safe and supportive environment where every student feels valued. Perspective-taking exercises can further develop empathy and compassion among students, promoting a more inclusive classroom culture.

IDEAS FOR THE CLASSROOM

Discuss real-life scenarios to initiate discussions on social influence and the challenges of making independent choices. Two examples of scenarios are given below.

1.   In your class, there's a new substitute teacher who is experiencing a lot of disruptive behaviour from the students. Whenever he tries to explain the work, there are constant interruptions and silliness. What actions can you take to help the situation?

2.   During a class game of Pictionary, a student has been asked to draw a picture on the board. Despite the picture being obvious, everyone remains silent and refuses to guess, making the student feel increasingly embarrassed. How can you respond to this situation and support your fellow classmate?

In each scenario, encourage empathy, kindness, and assertiveness among students, so they feel empowered to address challenging situations while promoting a positive and supportive classroom environment.

EMBEDDING SOCIAL AND EMOTIONAL SKILLS INTO THE CURRICULUM

When writing schemes of work, teachers can think about where they can teach the skills needed to resist negative social influence. Here are some ideas:

- *Educate students about the psychological processes underlying social influence*: By discussing influential studies like Asch's (1951) line study and Zimbardo's (1971) prison experiment, students become aware of the darker aspects of human behaviour and the importance of resisting negative pressures. Empower your students to be agents of positive change.

- *Teach critical thinking skills*: Students evaluate information and situations independently, question assumptions, seek evidence, and consider different perspectives before making a decision.

- *Teach media literacy*: Critically analyse media messages that often influence behaviours. Students should be aware of how to keep themselves safe from online influences. This information should be relevant and age appropriate.

- *Teach assertiveness and communication skills*: Enable students to express their boundaries confidently, have courageous conversations with others if needed, and identify when they might need help and how to access that help.

The table below considers what to do when having a courageous conversation.

Adhere to A DEAR	You're a good friend of mine and I know that I can speak to you about anything. You know earlier today when we got our Spanish test back and I got 98%. I heard you say, 'Of course she did well, her mum's Spanish!' That made me feel hurt because I worked hard for that test. It made me feel sad that people think that I am good at Spanish because of my mum. I know that you probably didn't mean to come across that way. Next time, please don't say things like that.
A: Affirm the person/relationship	
D: Describe the behaviour without judgement	
E: Explain the impact of that behaviour	
A: Assume positive intent.	
R: Request/suggest a different behaviour.	

(Continued)

(Continued)

Affirm the relationship.	I enjoy hanging out with you. You are so much fun. But sometimes, when you tease me because of my accent, I feel embarrassed and very uncomfortable because this is how I speak. Next time, please don't make fun of my accent. Thank you. I know that you would have wanted me to tell you because you probably wouldn't want me to feel this way. I think of you as a good friend.
When you...	
I feel...	
Next time...	
Assume positive intent and reaffirm the relationship	
Stop it.	For younger children, just saying 'Stop it, I don't like it' in an assertive tone might be enough to set boundaries.
I don't like it.	
What techniques do you use to have courageous conversations?	

 HINTS AND TIPS

It is equally important to teach students how to respond to these conversations when they are at the receiving end:

- **Listen with full attention.**

- **Don't respond/react straight away. Take deep breaths and acknowledge your feelings.**

- **Remember that your mistakes don't define you.**

- **Apologise for the impact of your behaviour (e.g. the hurt or the sadness).**

These are some useful statements:

'I am sorry that my words and actions made you feel that way.'

'Thank you for telling me.'

'I really don't know how I could have done it differently. Let me have a few minutes and maybe we can speak to someone about it?'

BUILDING SOCIAL SUPPORT

When there is social support, people can express their views more easily. For example, in Asch's (1951) study, conformity levels dropped from 32% to 5% when one of the actors gave the correct answer (social support). Some ways to help students to build social support include:

- *Provide role models*: Introduce students to inspiring role models – historical figures, celebrities, or even classmates who have demonstrated courage to resist harmful group pressure or used social influence to positively impact their communities.

- *Encourage students to engage with the broader community*: Involving parents, carers, and the wider school communities reinforces the importance of social norms that embrace the wellbeing of students. It allows students to experience a sense of belonging that enhances their overall wellbeing.

- *Create opportunities for student agency*: In my experience, often students have a fairly good understanding of the issues associated with their wellbeing. When teachers actively listen to student voices, it empowers students to lead discussions concerning their own wellbeing (Stones et al., 2020). Student-led events which highlight issues that relate to mental health are powerful ways of creating student agency.

 CASE STUDY

21ST CENTURY CHILD – ST MICHAEL'S CHURCH OF ENGLAND SCHOOL, WEST MIDLANDS, UK

21st Century Child is a programme centred around student voice (St Michael's Church of England High School, n.d.). The initiative

(Continued)

aims to raise awareness of issues affecting young people using innovative approaches. Meetings are held with stakeholders (students, parents, and teachers) to discuss areas of concern that need to be addressed. Then the student group together with relevant members of staff discuss the challenges and develop support strategies. These are presented by the students at engaging, and interactive events.

How events are structured depends on the issues and can be for students only or both students and parents, providing a platform for addressing challenging topics. The themes for events are determined by issues of concern to the students and developed through consultation with key stakeholders. Past events have focused on issues such as social media, body image, identity, mental health, and youth violence.

Student voice at St Michael's started out with just a few students. Now the initiative enjoys involvement and participation from a huge number of students across the school.

At a conference in July 2023, a 16-year-old student at St Michael's, remarked, 'As a former member and now ambassador, I can see how the student voice and our initiatives are shaping the next generation of mental health advocates and, on a broader scale, fostering more compassionate individuals in our school. Personally, it's been crucial for my own mental health journey, teaching me emotional literacy and resilience – things that the curriculum alone wouldn't have covered.'

The case study shows how student agency can enhance wellbeing, particularly through fostering meaning and relationships in the following ways:

- Involving students in decision-making empowers them and creates a sense of ownership and engagement. This results in meaningful participation and discussions on topics directly relevant to their lives, such as mental health and identity, promoting purpose.

- Student-led events provide a safe space for open expression, culti-vating trust and deeper connections with peers and parents during joint activities.

- Addressing current issues equips students with coping strategies and resources, empowering them to proactively safeguard their wellbeing.

- Collaborative efforts with professionals, organisations, and parents foster a supportive community and positive school climate, where students feel valued and supported.

This initiative is a great example of how social influence can be used to create a culture of wellbeing in the school community.

NOTE IT DOWN

FOR YOU

USE SOCIAL INFLUENCE TO SUPPORT YOUR COMMITMENT TO STUDENT MENTAL HEALTH – BY CONNECTING WITH LIKE-MINDED EDUCATORS IN YOUR SCHOOL OR ON SOCIAL MEDIA (OR BY FINDING OUT MORE INFORMATION FROM ORGANISATIONS SUCH AS MINDS AHEAD WHICH AIM TO RESHAPE MENTAL HEALTH IN EDUCATION. MAKE A LIST OF PEOPLE OR ORGANISATIONS WHO WILL REINFORCE YOUR COMMITMENT HERE:

FOR YOUR STUDENTS

HOW CAN YOU USE FOSTER STUDENT AGENCY IN YOUR SCHOOL TO EMPOWER STUDENTS TO MAKE A POSITIVE CONTRIBUTION TO THEIR SCHOOL COMMUNITY? JOT DOWN YOUR IDEAS BELOW.

CHAPTER 6

ASSESSING WELLBEING

LOCATING STUDENTS AND PROGRESSING THEM ALONG THE WELLBEING GRADIENT

This chapter covers:

- A discussion of methods for identifying students who may be struggling, coping, or thriving in the classroom
- The three factors of promoting mental health in education
- Further resources for educators to integrate wellbeing into their teaching practice

> *The measure of who we are is what we do*
> *with what we have.*
> Vince Lombardi

Earlier chapters in this book have described theories of wellbeing and strategies to enhance mental health. Once some of these ideas have been implemented, it is helpful to evaluate the outcomes.

THE STUDENT WELLBEING GRADIENT

In the classroom, teachers can use qualitative measures to assess wellbeing. It is helpful to have some ways of identifying when students might be struggling, when they are just coping (Muhammad et al., 2012) and when they are thriving (Lerner et al., 2005; Langridge et al, 2022). 'Struggling', 'coping', and 'thriving' are concepts that have been described by others. These are not discrete states, but rather a continuum which I will refer to as the 'student wellbeing gradient'. Distinguishing between these states involves assessing various aspects of a student's academic, emotional, and social wellbeing. This is a process that will be referred to as 'locating student positions along the wellbeing gradient'.

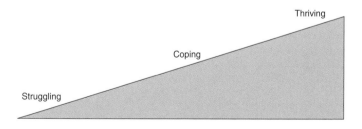

Locating students on the wellbeing gradient requires a holistic approach. Of course, there might be individual differences, but it might be a worthwhile exercise to create a list of behaviours to help guide your practice. For example, I have summarised some general guidelines on how teachers may be able to assess if their students are struggling, coping, or thriving in the following table below.

	Struggling Pupils	Students Coping/ Surviving	Thriving Students
Emotions	- Difficulty coping with difficult emotions: Signs of frustration, anxiety, sadness. May not cope with failure or know their strengths.	- Generally stable emotions, moderate school-related stress or joy. Aware of strengths but may not use them for wellbeing.	- High level of positive emotions related to learning. Enthusiastic and curious. Aware of strengths and use them for wellbeing and others'.
Engagement	- Lack of engagement: Disinterest, trouble concentrating, reluctance to seek help.	- Engage as needed but may do the bare minimum.	- Intrinsically motivated, actively engage in learning, display a growth mindset.
Social Interaction	- Limited social interaction, struggles to make meaningful connections.	- Maintain moderate social interaction, may not seek out opportunities.	- Maintain positive relationships with peers and teachers. Contribute positively to the classroom environment.

(Continued)

(Continued)

Behavioural Issues	-	Behavioural problems: Acting out, disruptive, avoidance of schoolwork. May not follow school rules.	-	May not explore additional learning opportunities or extracurricular activities.	-	Take initiative to explore new topics, participate in extracurricular activities, seek personal development opportunities.
Academic Challenges	-	Academic difficulties: Lower grades, incomplete assignments, below-average test scores.	-	Meet minimum academic requirements but may not excel or show enthusiasm.	-	Complete classwork and homework, show enjoyment of learning.

 # REFLECTION

How do you identify students who might be struggling, coping, or thriving in your classroom?

Wellbeing is a process, and it is personal to each individual. It is important to note that students may move in both directions along the gradient over time, and individual circumstances can vary widely. A holistic approach, including classroom observations, academic performance assessments, conversations with students, and collaboration with other school staff members and parents will help teachers gain a comprehensive understanding of each student's wellbeing and tailor support accordingly. Additionally, teachers should consider the unique strengths and challenges that each student has. Providing targeted interventions when needed will help struggling students move towards coping and thriving.

PROMOTING MENTAL HEALTH: THREE FACTORS

As we work towards supporting our students' wellbeing in the hope of preparing them to face challenges, three elements are fundamental in helping students move up the wellbeing gradient, no matter their current location:

1. *Teaching skills for mental health*: We need to teach our students skills that they need for mental health and fitness. These skills will not only build up their resilience to effectively deal with difficulties but also help them to recover more quickly when they face challenges. The skills include goal setting, accurate assessment of the demands that they face and the resources available to them to deal with those demands, dealing with failure, and managing difficult emotions.

2. *Opportunities for regular practice*: Knowing these skills is important but practice is equally crucial. Creating opportunities for regular practice will help our students develop habits of mental fitness. We should provide our students with opportunities to exercise the skills of mental health outlined in this book. For example, students can practise strength spotting within their families, in their classrooms, in the school community, and in society. Helping students use their skills in valued contexts such as these will help them gain a sense of purpose. By making a positive contribution to their environment, students will strengthen their own mental health.

3. *Nurturing relationships*: One of the most powerful assets in fostering student wellbeing is the quality of relationships we build with our students. Relationships with competent and compassionate teachers who are committed to supporting the wellbeing can do wonders for a child's mental health.

The value of the three factors is emphasised by developmental psychologist Richard Lerner (2009) who asserts that all young people can thrive if they have a sustained positive relationship with at least one teacher who focuses on their strengths. This coupled with opportunities to contribute positively to their communities can enhance the chances of students developing their resilience (Geldhof, 2013).

HINTS AND TIPS

Remember, to help students move up the wellbeing gradient, teachers can do a *TON*!

T: Teach the skills

O: Opportunities to practise the skills

N: Nurturing relationships to provide guidance, support, and encouragement

REFLECTION

Teachers can offer various avenues for students to practise their skills. These include:

- Academic and extracurricular enrichment activities

- Calm/quiet spaces for reflection

- Platforms for self-expression (using pupil voice)

- Opportunities to build student–teacher relationships beyond the classroom (e.g. school trips, participating in activities together like choir or drama)

What are some ways that you can provide opportunities for your students?

EMBEDDING WELLBEING INTO YOUR DAILY PRACTICE

The greatest glory in living lies not in never Falling, but in rising every time we Fall.
Nelson Mandela

With the increasing concern surrounding children's mental health, educators are faced with a significant challenge. I hope that this toolkit has provided you with valuable resources to assist you in responding to this call to action. Which ones you choose to experiment with and implement in your teaching practice will depend on your unique context. Not every approach will work the same way for every student or classroom, and that's perfectly okay. The key is to remain flexible and open to adaptation, always guided by the intention of improving the wellbeing of your students.

Wellbeing is mutually influential and beneficial. As you help your students flourish, you'll likely find that your own wellbeing improves as well due to its ripple effect. By integrating wellbeing practices into every aspect of your job, from lesson planning to report writing, you will help each of your students to 'realise his or her own abilities, cope with the normal stresses of life, work productively and fruitfully and make a contribution to his or her community' (World Health Organization, 2022). You will make a positive contribution to the overall health and wellbeing of your students, your school community, and society as a whole.

Good luck!

NOTE IT DOWN

As educators, we need to be able to examine various theories and resources, test them out within our own contexts and assess how we measure the impact on our students' lives. Only then can we evaluate their worth. If a strategy works, we make it part of our practice; if it doesn't, we tweak it or rethink it entirely. If we are to effectively support the wellbeing of our students, we need to use a systematic and scientific approach.

1. Identify a realistic strategy that you would like to try out.

2. Plan:

   A. Exactly what will you do and why

   B. How will you know if it is working? How long will you try it out for?

   C. What resources will you need?

3. Implement that strategy. Keep a journal so that you can monitor the impact.

4. Check for effectiveness. Has it made a positive difference?

   A. If yes, how will you embed it in your teaching practice?

   B. If no, can you tweak the strategy and try again? Can you use a different strategy?

   C. Did you learn anything else that could inform your work?

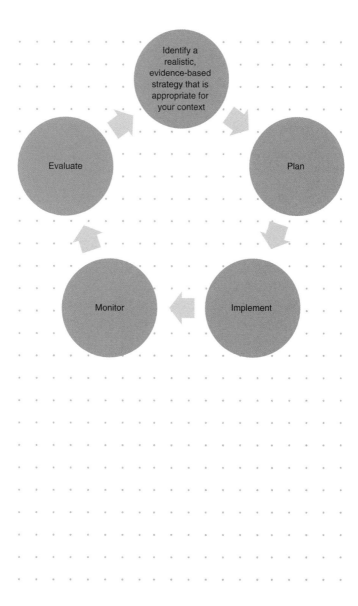

FURTHER RESOURCES

Below is a compilation of additional resources. These include guidance from educational organisations, books, TED Talks, and websites that offer valuable insights and practical tools to integrate wellbeing into teaching practice.

Department for Education (2021) *Mental health and wellbeing resources for teachers and teaching staff*. https://assets.publishing.service. gov.uk/media/63453e208fa8f534695f3984/Mental_health_ resources_for_teachers_and_teaching_staff.pdf

HM Government (2021) *Promoting children and young people's mental health and wellbeing: A whole school or college approach*. Public Health England and DfE. https://assets.publishing.service.gov.uk/ media/614cc965d3bf7f718518029c/Promoting_children_and_ young_people_s_mental_health_and_wellbeing.pdf

NHS England

Mental health support in schools and colleges. www.england.nhs.uk/ mental-health/cyp/trailblazers

Anna Freud is a charity dedicated to providing support and training for children's mental health. Their *Classroom wellbeing toolkit* contains more practical tips on embedding wellbeing into everyday teaching practice. www.annafreud.org/resources/schools-and-colleges/ classroom-wellbeing-toolkit

The **World Health Organization's** publication *Mental Health in Schools: A Manual* is packed with useful resources for children of all ages. Available at: https://applications.emro.who.int/ docs/9789290225652-eng.pdf

The **Carnegie School of Education** at Leeds Becket University has put together a framework for schools (and other educational institutions) to evidence strategies that improve emotional health and wellbeing for staff and pupils. Applying for a School Mental Health Award (Bronze, Silver or Gold) has many benefits including support to make wellbeing a strategic priority by working with an allocated coach to create a personalised action plan. Visit the website for more information. www.leedsbeckett.ac.uk/carnegie-school-of-education

Action for Happiness is an excellent charity which provides lots of ideas and resources. I love using the resources, particularly attending the talks by wellbeing experts around the world, to enhance my own wellbeing knowledge. https://actionfor happiness.org

Young Minds and **Place2Be** are mental health charities that have useful resources for children, young people, and their parents. www.youngminds.org.uk and www.place2be.org.uk.

Well Schools www.well-school.org

IDEAS FOR ASSEMBLIES, PSHE, AND TUTOR TIME

Greater Good in Education is an organisation in the USA whose website has evidence-backed ideas for bringing wellbeing into schools. It has resources that are applicable to students of all ages. https://ggie.berkeley.edu

Character Lab is another great resource. It includes playbooks – guides to cultivate strengths and tips – 60 seconds of actionable advice based on science. https://characterlab.org

JOURNALS

Mental Health Insights is a fantastic resource because it has lots of think pieces, case studies of practical strategies used by educators, and book reviews focusing on mental health in schools. www.leeds-beckett.ac.uk/research/carnegie-centre-of-excellence-for-mental-health-in-schools/working-paper-series

Impact is a termly journal that is available to members of the Chartered College of Teaching and has a wellbeing section. Articles in this journal are high quality, practical, and relevant to educators.

BOOKS

Adrian Bethune and Emma Kell (2020) *A Little Guide for Teachers: Teacher Wellbeing*. Sage Publications.

Bennie Kara (2020) *A Little Guide for Teachers: Diversity in Schools*. Sage Publications.

Susan David (2017) *Emotional agility: Get unstuck, embrace change and thrive in work and life*. Penguin.

Shirzad Chamene (2012) *Positive intelligence: Why only 20% of teams and individuals achieve their true potential and how you can achieve yours*. Greenleaf Book Group.

TED TALKS AND DOCUMENTARIES WHICH LINK WELL WITH THE SPECIFIC CHAPTERS

Chapter 1	Shawn Achor – The happy secret to better work
	Martin Seligman – The new era of positive psychology
Chapter 2	Rita Pierson – Every kid needs a champion
	Shane Lopez – Focusing on your strengths
	Peter Benson – Sparks: How youth thrive.
Chapter 3	Kelly McGonigal – How to make stress your friend
	Susan David – The gift and power of emotional courage
	Andy Puddicombe – All it takes is 10 mindful minutes
Chapter 4	Angela Duckworth – The power of passion and perseverance.
	Behrouz Moemeni – Intrinsic motivation: The key to revolutionize education, work and life
	Dan Pink – The puzzle of motivation
Chapter 5	Stanley Milgram – The Milgram Experiment 1962
	YouTube – Heroic Imagination Project

REFERENCES

Achor, S. (2011). *The happiness advantage: The seven principles of positive psychology that fuel success and performance at work*. Random House.

Al-Harthy, I. S. (2016). Contemporary motivation learning theories: A review. *International Journal of Learning Management Systems*, *4*(2), 99–117.

Asch, S. E. (1951). Effects of group pressure on the modification and distortion of judgments. In H. Guetzkow (Ed.), *Groups, leadership and men* (pp. 177–190). Carnegie Press.

Authentic Happiness (2023). Website, www.authentichappiness.sas.upenn.edu

Banks, T., & Zionts, P. (2009). Teaching a cognitive behavioral strategy to manage emotions: Rational emotive behavior therapy in an educational setting. *Intervention in School and Clinic*, *44*(5), 307–313.

Battistich, V., Schaps, E., & Wilson, N. (2004). Effects of an elementary school intervention on students' 'connectedness' to school and social adjustment during middle school. *Journal of Primary Prevention*, *24*, 243–262.

Bawuro, F. A., Shamsuddin, A., Wahab, E., & Usman, H. (2019). Mediating role of meaningful work in the relationship between intrinsic motivation and innovative work behaviour. *International Journal of Scientific and Technology Research*, *8*(9), 2076–2084.

Brownlee, K., Rawana, E. P., & MacArthur, J. (2012). Implementation of a strengths-based approach to teaching in an elementary school. *Journal of Teaching and Learning*, *8*(1), https://jtl.uwindsor.ca/index.php/jtl/article/view/3069

Chamine, S. (2012). *Positive intelligence: Why only 20% of teams and individuals achieve their true potential and how you can achieve yours.* Greenleaf Book Group.

Corcoran, F., & Whitehead, S. (2021). Exploring character and supporting well-being with Frida Kahlo and Albert Einstein. In K. Evans, T. Hoyle, F. Roberts, & B. Yusuf (Eds), *The big book of whole school well-being* (pp. 1–100). Corwin.

Csikszentmihályi, M. (1990). The domain of creativity. In M. A. Runco & R. S. Albert (Eds), *Theories of creativity* (pp. 190–212). Sage Publications.

David, S. (2016). *Emotional agility: Get unstuck, embrace change, and thrive in work and life*. Penguin.

David, S. (2021). Emotional granularity checklists. www.susandavid.com/resource/emotional-checklist-general

Davidson, R. (2012). *The emotional life of your brain: How its unique patterns affect the way you think, feel, and live – and how you can change them.* Penguin.

Deci, E. L., & Ryan, R. M. (1985). *Intrinsic motivation and self-determination in human behaviour*. Plenum Press.

Department for Education (2023) *Keeping children safe in education 2023: Statutory guidance for schools and colleges.* https://assets.publishing.service.gov.uk/government/uploads/system/uploads/attachment_data/file/1181955/Keeping_children_safe_in_education_2023.pdf

Duckworth, A. (2013). The power of passion and perseverance. TED Talk. www.youtube.com/watch?v=H14bBuluwB8

Duckworth, A. L., Peterson, C., Matthews, M. D., & Kelly, D. R. (2007). Grit: Perseverance and passion for long-term goals. *Journal of Personality and Social Psychology*, *92*(6), 1087–1101.

Dweck, C. S. (2008). Brainology: Transforming students' motivation to learn. *Independent School*, *67*(2), 110–119.

Elias, M. J., Ogburn-Thompson, G., Lewis, C., & Neft, D. I. (Eds) (2007). *Urban dreams: Stories of hope, resilience and character*. Hamilton Books.

Ellis, A. (1991). The revised ABC's of rational-emotive therapy (RET). *Journal of Rational-Emotive and Cognitive-Behavior Therapy*, *9*(3), 139–172.

Falecki, D., Leach, C., & Green, S. (2018). PERMA-powered coaching: Building foundations for a flourishing life. In S. Green & S. Palmer (Eds), *Positive psychology coaching in practice* (pp. 103–116). Routledge.

Galloway, R., Reynolds, B., & Williamson, J. (2020). Strengths-based teaching and learning approaches for children: Perceptions and practices. *Journal of Pedagogical Research*, *4*(1), 31–45.

Gandhi, P., & Outhwaite, D. (2023). Applying the science of learning in secondary school classrooms: A case study of a 'Psychology for Learning' course for Year 9 students. Impact, https://my.chartered.college/impact_article/applying-the-science-of-learning-in-secondary-school-classrooms-a-case-study-of-a-psychology-for-learning-course-for-year-9-students

Geldhof, G. J., Bowers, E. P., & Lerner, R. M. (2013). Special section introduction: Thriving in context: Findings from the 4-H study of positive youth development. *Journal of Youth and Adolescence*, *42*, 1–5.

Independent Mental Health Taskforce to the NHS in England (2016). The Five Year Forward View for Mental Health. Available at: www.england.nhs.uk/wp-content/uploads/2016/02/Mental-Health-Taskforce-FYFV-final.pdf

Jung, C. G. (1921). *Psychologische typen*. Rascher Verlag.

Juslin, P. N., & Sakka, L. S. (2019). Neural correlates of music and emotion. In M. H. Thaut & D. A. Hodges (Eds), *The Oxford handbook of music and the brain* (pp. 285–332). Oxford University Press.

Langridge, F. C., Ofanoa, M., Fakakovikaetau, T., Wilkinson-Meyers, L., Percival, T., Riley, A. W. & Grant, C. C. (2022). Surviving versus thriving: The wellbeing of primary school aged children in Tonga. *Journal of Paediatrics and Child Health*, *58*(5), 880–886.

Lazarus, R. S., DeLongis, A., Folkman, S., & Gruen, R. (1985). Stress and adaptational outcomes: The problem of confounded measures. *American Psychologist*, *40*(7), 770–779.

Lerner, R. M. (2009). The positive youth development perspective: Theoretical and empirical bases of a strengths-based approach to adolescent development. In S. J. Lopez & C. R. Snyder (Eds), *The Oxford handbook of positive psychology* (pp. 149–164). Oxford University Press.

Lerner, R. M., Almerigi, J. B., Theokas, C., & Lerner, J. V. (2005). Positive youth development: A view of the issues. *The Journal of Early Adolescence*, *25*(1), 10–16.

Linley, P. A., Nielsen, K. M., Gillett, R., & Biswas-Diener, R. (2010). Using signature strengths in pursuit of goals: Effects on goal progress, need satisfaction, and well-being, and implications for coaching psychologists. *International Coaching Psychology Review*, *5*(1), 6–15.

Locke, E. A., & Latham, G. P. (2002). Building a practically useful theory of goal setting and task motivation: A 35-year odyssey. *American Psychologist*, *57*(9), 705–717.

Lyubomirsky, S., King, L., & Diener, E. (2005). The benefits of frequent positive affect: Does happiness lead to success? *Psychological Bulletin*, *131*(6), 803–855.

Maslow, A., & Lewis, K. J. (1987). Maslow's hierarchy of needs. *Salenger*, *14*(17), 987–990.

McGonigal, K. (2013). How to make stress your friend. TED Global. Available at: www.voicetube.com/videos/8236

Muhammad, S., Banks, P., & Martin, C. R. (2012). Coping: Is this the foundation of wellbeing? A narrative review. *British Journal of Mental Health Nursing*, *1*(4), 224–231.

National Careers Service. The STAR method. Available at: https://nationalcareers.service.gov.uk/careers-advice/interview-advice/the-star-method

NHS Digital (2021). Mental Health of Children and Young People in England, 2021. Available at: https://files.digital.nhs.uk/97/B09EF8/mhcyp_2021_rep.pdf

Niemiec, R. M., & McGrath, R. E. (2019). The power of character strengths: Appreciate and ignite your positive personality. VIA Institute on Character.

Oettingen, G. (2012). Future thought and behavior change. *European Review of Social Psychology*, *23*(1), 1–63.

Peterson, C., & Seligman, M. E. (2004). *Character strengths and virtues: A handbook and classification* (Vol. 1). Oxford University Press.

Pierson, R. (2013). Every kid needs a champion. TED Talks Education. www.ted.com/talks/rita_pierson_every_kid_needs_a_champion?language=en

Pineda, K. The Importance of Being Seen – Humantold. Available at: https://humantold.com/blog/the-importance-of-being-seen/ (accessed 25/7/2023).

Reupert, A., Straussner, S.L., Weirmand, B., & Maybery, D. (2022). It takes a village to raise a child: Understanding and expanding the concept of the 'village'. *Frontiers*, 10, https://doi.org/10.3389/fpubh.2022.756066

Ryan, R. M., & Deci, E. L. (2000). Self-determination theory and the facilitation of intrinsic motivation, social development, and well-being. *American Psychologist*, *55*(1), 68–78.

Ryan, R. M., & Deci, E. L. (2017). *Self-determination theory: Basic psychological needs in motivation, development, and wellness*. Guilford Press.

Seligman, M. E. (2011). *Flourish: A visionary new understanding of happiness and well-being*. Simon & Schuster.

Seligman, M. (2018). PERMA and the building blocks of well-being. *The Journal of Positive Psychology*, *13*(4), 333–335.

Shernoff, D. J., & Csikszentmihalyi, M. (2009). Cultivating engaged learners and optimal learning environments. In R. Gilman, E. S. Huebner & M. Furlong (Eds), *Handbook of Positive Psychology in Schools* (pp. 211–226). Routledge.

Sinek, S. (2011). *Start with why: How great leaders inspire everyone to take action*. Penguin.

Smiling Mind. www.smilingmind.com.au/ (accessed 6/10/23).

St Michael's Church of England High School. 21st Century Child. Available at: https://st-michaels.sandwell.sch.uk/21st-century-child/

Stones, S., Glazzard, J., & Muzio, M. R. (Eds) (2020). *Selected topics in child and adolescent mental health*. BoD – Books on Demand.

Treasure, J. (2011). 5 ways to listen better. TED Conferences. Available at: www.ted.com/talks/julian_treasure_5_ways_to_listen_better?language=en (accessed 3/2/ 2023).

Vansteenkiste, M., Sierens, E., Soenens, B., Luyckx, K., & Lens, W. (2009). Motivational profiles from a self-determination perspective: The quality of motivation matters. *Journal of Educational Psychology*, *101*(3), 671–688.

Weare, K. (2013). *Promoting mental, emotional and social health: A whole school approach*. Routledge.

World Health Organization (2022). Mental Health Key Facts. Available at: www.who.int/news-room/fact-sheets/detail/mental-health-strengthening-our-response

Zimbardo, P. G., Haney, C., Banks, W. C., & Jaffe, D. (1971). *The Stanford prison experiment*. The US Office of Naval Research.

INDEX

21st Century Child programme, 67–68

ABCD model of stress management, 36, 37
accomplishment, celebrating, 12, 24–26
Achor, Shawn, 6–7
Action for Happiness (charity), 84
agency, 67–69, 72
Ali, Muhammad, 26
Anna Freud (charity), 83
Asch, Solomon, 60, 67
Authentic Happiness (website), 21
autonomy, 27, 53, 54

belonging, sense of, 8–9, 18, 22, 67
blind obedience, 61, 62tab
boundary-setting, 27
breathing, and mindfulness, 42

celebrations and rewards
    achievements, 12, 24–26
    character strengths, 23, 24–26, 63
    diversity, 63
    and motivation, 47–48
    STAR framework, 24–26
Chamine, Shirzad, 42
character strengths see
        strengths-based approach
Classroom wellbeing toolkit, 83
cognitive restructuring (stress
        management tool), 36–37

communication skills
    courageous conversations, 65,
        65–66tab, 66–67
    listening, 10, 18–19
competence, 12, 27, 54
confidence-building, 19, 24, 54,
    62, 63
conformity, 60–61, 62tab, 67
connectedness, 8–9, 18
control see autonomy
conversations, courageous, 65,
    65–66tab, 66–67
COVID-19 pandemic, 1–2, 50
creativity, 8, 12, 33
critical thinking skills, 65
curiosity, 22, 28, 48

David, Susan, 37–38
Davidson, Richard, 6
deindividuation, 61, 62tab
diet and nutrition, 13, 46
displays in the classroom
    character strengths, 22
    growth mindset, 53
diversity, 19, 63
Duckworth, Angela, 50–52

Ellis, Albert, 36
emotions
    positive, 6–8, 39fig
    self-regulation, 21, 22, 37–38, 41,
        43, 47, 53, 77
    stress see stress

vocabulary and granularity,
38–41, 39fig
and wellbeing gradient, 75tab
empathy, 10, 18–19, 36–37, 63
'The Emperor's New Clothes' (conformity example), 60
engagement, 8, 68, 75tab
exercise, 13, 46
extracurricular activities, 76tab, 78
extrinsic motivation, 47–48
see also motivation

failure, learning from, 52, 77
see also growth mindset
fight, flight or freeze stress
response, 33, 34tab
'flow' state, 8

games, 8
goal-setting, 12–13, 23, 77
gratitude journals, 6–7
grit, 50–52
see also perseverance
group work, 9, 25, 55
and social influence, 61, 62tab
growth mindset, 48, 52–53
see also curiosity; failure,
learning from

The Happiness Advantage, 6–7
hierarchy of needs, 46

inclusivity, 18–19, 22
intrinsic motivation, 47–55, 75tab
see also motivation

Jordan, Michael, 52
journals
achievements, 26
for developing perseverance, 23

gratitude, 6–7
reflective (teachers), 3, 80
see also reflective writing
(students)
Jung, Carl, 37

Keeping Children Safe in Education
(KCSIE), 46

leadership skills, 22
learning theories, teaching to
students, 54
Lerner, Richard, 77
life satisfaction, 22
listening skills, 10, 18–19
Lombardi, Vince, 74

Mandela, Nelson, 78
Maslow, Abraham, 46
McGonigal, Kelly, 35–36
meaning and purpose, 11–12, 48–50
media literacy skills, 65
mental fitness see wellbeing
mental health see wellbeing
mental health referrals, 13
mindfulness, 41–43
motivation
blind obedience and, 62tab
definition, 46
extrinsic, 47–48
feeling 'seen' and, 18
growth mindset and, 48, 52–53
intrinsic, 47–55, 75tab
meaning and, 11, 48–50
music and, 8
needs and, 46–47
rewards and, 47–48
self-determination theory and, 53–56
self-efficacy and, 12
music, 8

needs, hierarchy of, 46
NHS Digital, 1–2
nutrition, 13, 46

online literacy and safety, 47, 65

parents
    collaborations with, 68, 69
    conversations with, 27
peer pressure *see* social influence
PERMA (Positive Emotion,
        Engagement, Relationships,
        Meaning, Accomplishment)
        theory of wellbeing, 6–15
perseverance, 22, 23, 51
perspective
    as character strength, 23
    of others, acknowledgement of,
        10, 37, 55, 63, 65
    'sage' perspective, 43–44
    validation of, 18
Pierson, Rita, 57
Place2Be (charity), 84
positive emotions, 6–8, 39fig
PQ (positive intelligence quotient)
        reps, 42
praise *see* celebrations and rewards
presentations, 23, 25
prosocial behaviours and skills,
        63–67
psychological fitness *see* wellbeing
purpose and meaning, 11–12, 48–50

RASA (Receive, Appreciate,
        Summarise, Ask questions)
        listening method, 10
reflective journals (teachers), 3, 80
reflective writing (students), 50, 54
relatedness, 27, 54, 55
relationships

belonging, 8–9, 18, 22, 67
    empathy and, 37
    student-student relationships,
        8–9, 22, 62–63, 75tab
    student-teacher relationships, 10,
        75tab, 77, 78
rewards *see* celebrations and
        rewards
role models
    other people as, 22, 67
    students as, 63, 67
    teachers as, 27

safeguarding guidance, 46
'sage' perspective, 43–44
School Mental Health Award, 83–84
SEA (Spot, Explain, Appreciate)
        strengths framework, 22–23
'seen,' being/feeling, 18–19
self-determination theory (SDT), 27,
        53–56
self-efficacy, 12
self-regulation, 21, 22, 37–38, 41,
        43, 47, 53, 77
Seligman, Martin, 6, 8, 13
Sinek, Simon, 48
sleep, 13, 46
SMART (Specific, Measurable,
        Realistic, Time-bound) goals, 12
social influence
    blind obedience, 61, 62tab
    conformity, 60–61, 62tab, 67
    deindividuation, 61, 62tab
    positive (social support), 67–69
    prosocial behaviours and skills,
        63–67
social interaction *see*
        communication skills;
        relatedness; relationships
social support, 67–69

STAR (Situation, Task, Action, Result)
      framework, 24–26
Start with Why, 48
strengths-based approach, 19–29,
      20tab, 63, 76, 77
stress
   definition and causes,
      32–33
   managing stress, 35–44, 39fig
   physiological and behavioural
      manifestations, 32, 33–34,
      34tab
   positive and optimum
      stress, 33
student voices, 67–69

targets *see* goal-setting
TED talks, 51, 57, 85tab
Treasure, Julian, 10

Urban Dreams: Stories of Hope,
      Resilience and Character, 50

validation, 18–19
values, 49–50

      see also meaning and purpose
VIA (Values in Action) survey, 21

wellbeing
   definition (WHO), 2
   gradient (struggling/coping/
      thriving), 74–75, 74fig,
      75–76tab, 76
   PERMA theory, 6–15
   planning for, 80, 82fig
   resources, 83–85
   self-determination theory, 27,
      53–56
   strategies for (overview),
      77–78
WOOP (Wish, Outcome, Obstacle,
      Plan) goals, 12
World Health Organization (WHO),
      1, 2, 46, 79

Yerkes-Dodson law of stress/
      performance, 33
Young Minds (charity), 84

Zimbardo, Philip, 61